W9-CTU-144

BOOKWORMS

Go, Critter, Go!
Fly, Butterfly, Fly!

¡Vamos criaturita, vamos!
¡Vuela mariposa, vuela!

Dana Meachen Rau

Marshall Cavendish
Benchmark
New York

Butterflies have
four wings.

———◆———

Las mariposas tienen
cuatro alas.

3

Butterflies have
six legs.

Las mariposas tienen
seis patas.

Butterflies have lots
of colors.

———————— ◆ ————————

Las mariposas tienen
muchos colores.

Butterflies start as caterpillars.

---◆---

Primero, las mariposas son orugas.

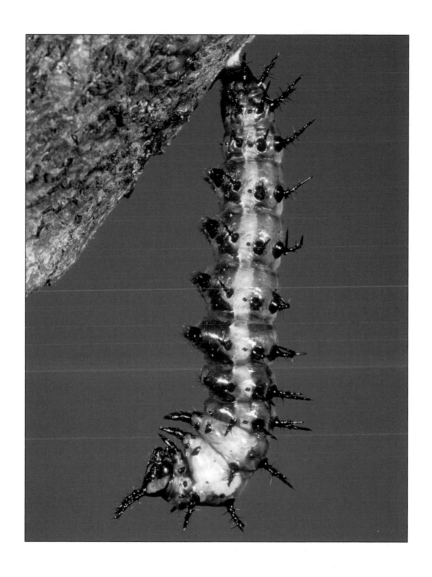

9

Caterpillars turn into butterflies.

---◆---

Las orugas se convierten en mariposas.

Butterflies sit on flowers.

---◆---

Las mariposas se posan en las flores.

Butterflies drink from flowers.

Las mariposas beben de las flores.

Butterflies fly.

———————◆———————

Las mariposas vuelan.

Fly, butterfly, fly!

¡Vuela mariposa, vuela!

Words We Know
Palabras conocidas

caterpillar
oruga

colors
colores

drink
beben

flowers
flores

20

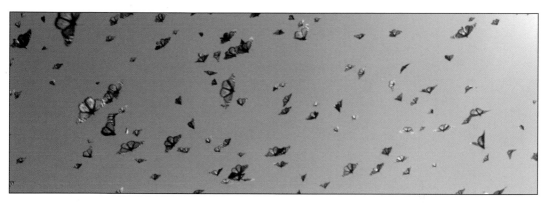

fly
vuelan

legs
patas

wings
alas

Index

Índice

About the Author

Dana Meachen Rau is an author, editor, and illustrator. A graduate of Trinity College in Hartford, Connecticut, she has written more than one hundred fifty books for children, including nonfiction, biographies, early readers, and historical fiction. She lives with her family in Burlington, Connecticut.

With thanks to the Reading Consultants:
Nanci Vargus, Ed.D., is an Assistant Professor of Elementary Education at the University of Indianapolis.

Beth Walker Gambro received her M.S. Ed. Reading from the University of St. Francis, Joliet, Illinois.

Sobre la autora

Dana Meachen Rau es escritora, editora e ilustradora. Graduada del Trinity College de Hartford, Connecticut, ha escrito más de ciento cincuenta libros para niños, entre ellos libros de ficción histórica y de no ficción, biografías y libros de lectura para principiantes. Vive con su familia en Burlington, Connecticut.

Con agradecimiento a las asesoras de lectura:
Nanci R. Vargus, Dra. en Ed., es profesora ayudante de educación primaria en la Universidad de Indianápolis.

Beth Walker Gambro recibió su Maestría en Ciencias de la Educación, con especialización en Lectura, de la Universidad de St. Francis, en Joliet, Illinois.

Marshall Cavendish Benchmark
99 White Plains Road
Tarrytown, New York 10591-9001
www.marshallcavendish.us

Library of Congress Cataloging-in-Publication Data

Rau, Dana Meachen, 1971–
[Fly, butterfly, fly! Spanish & English]
Fly, butterfly, fly! = ¡Vuela mariposa, vuela! / by Dana Meachen Rau.
p. cm. – (Go, critter, go! / ¡Vamos criaturita, vamos!)
Includes index.
ISBN-13: 978-0-7614-2814-5 (bilingual edition) – ISBN-13: 978-0-7614-2790-2 (spanish edition)
ISBN-13: 978-0-7614-2649-3 (english edition)
1. Butterflies–Juvenile literature.
I. Title. II. Title: ¡Vuela mariposa, vuela!
QL544.2.R38518 2007b
595.78'9–dc22
2007013902

Spanish Translation and Text Composition by
Victory Productions, Inc.

Photo Research by Anne Burns Images

Cover Photo by *Animals Animals*/Stephen Dalton

The photographs in this book are used with permission and through the courtesy of:
Corbis: pp. 1, 19 Fritz Rauschenback/zefa; pp. 3, 21BR Laura Sivell/Papilio; pp. 13, 20BR Darrell Gulin;
pp. 17, 21T James L. Amos. *Animals Animals*: pp. 5, 7, 20TR, 21BL Fabio Medeiros Columbini;
pp. 9, 11, 20TL Patti Murray; pp. 15, 20BL Arthur Evans.

Printed in Malaysia
1   3   5   6   4   2